TO: MAAME
WITH LOTS OT
FROM ME
GOD BLESS YOU.

GW01402663

The Power In
the Names of God

by

Gilbert M Asare

Grosvenor House
Publishing Limited

This book is published by
Grosvenor House Publishing Ltd
28-30 High Street, Guildford, Surrey, GU1 3EL.
www.grosvenorhousepublishing.co.uk

A CIP record for this book
is available from the British Library

ISBN 978-1-78148-512-5

DEDICATION

In writing this book, there has been no doubt about where the source of my inspiration and strength lay. God the Father through his Son Jesus Christ by the power of the Holy Ghost has taken me through this spiritual endeavour with great love and care. God gave me the vision and the strength to write this book. I owe everything in this piece of work to God's plan and purpose in my life. He has given me a transformation in my life and also cause to hope for eternal life by His grace and mercy. I therefore dedicate this book to God the Father, God the Son, and God the Holy Spirit. Amen.

CONTENTS

ACKNOWLEDGEMENTS

My thanks also go to the following for their unflinching support towards me. To my wife evangelist Mrs Christina Asare, I very much appreciate the spiritual, moral and material support that you offered me. It really gave me the much needed encouragement to pursue this goal.

To my great brothers in the Lord; Pastor Atsu Tettevi and Mr Robert Appiah Kwarteng, thank you for reading through the manuscript and making very useful suggestions.

To Ms Lisa Georghiades, I say thank you for your initial proof reading which has gone a long way to help shape this finishing product. I also want to thank Paul Gibbons for his excellent skills as a courier.

To my spiritual parents Reverend Martin Meder and Mrs Katharine Meder, I say thank you for your continued spiritual and moral support offered to me whenever I have had to call on you. Thank you for reading through the manuscript and offering very useful suggestions.

To my parents Opanin Samuel Baden Mprah and Mrs Susanna Lartebea Mprah I continue to thank God for your lives, for your vision and tenacity in bringing me up the way you did. I will forever be grateful to you. My heart's desire is this piece of work will inspire you to know Jesus better.

To my children Gabrielle, Emmanuel, Stefan and Michaela it is my sincere desire that this book will inspire you to offer yourselves as living sacrifices for the LORD.

Sister Joyce Ababio, may the Almighty God richly bless you for your extraordinary spirit of generosity. Your act of giving is exemplary. The LORD has really used you to bless our ministry and the work in His Kingdom.

I also have the pleasure to thank the members of the Crown of Glory Church, UK; the Crown of Glory Pentecostal Church, Ghana; and also members of Radio El Gibbor and Mighty God Radio, especially the precious sponsors worldwide for your support and encouragement.

To Micky Manu thank you for your patience, expertise and generosity in designing the front and back cover for this book. I also owe you a great debt of gratitude for doing the same for my first book *THE DAMAGE OF MURMURING TO THE BELIEVER*.

All scripture verses used in this book are from The New Open Bible, King James Version, Large Print Edition, and The King James Bible Red Lettered Special Margin Edition.

However it must be noted that I am fully responsible for the entire contents of this book.

FOREWORD

The name of a person is an important part of his being and must be taken seriously. A name reveals a person's character and gives a unique sense of his individuality, his attributes, and his values. The study of God's name is important for the believer if we are to know Him in a full and meaningful sense.

In this book, Reverend Gilbert Asare gives each believer a unique opportunity to have a first-hand experience encounter and a clear- cut understanding of the names of God and their implication for our daily existence. He explains that having a clear knowledge and understanding of the names of God does greatly reward a believer. He makes it clear that such knowledge moulds both our own faith and character, and moves our heart in a worshipful experience. Our names are precious to us, and the man of God makes it clear that it is important to know our God and His name, for, the more you get to know a person, the more you get acquainted well enough to use their nick names or their private exclusive names which other less acquainted individuals may not have the privilege to use. God wants us to have a greater level of holy familiarity as well as an in-depth and intense, intimate relationship with him which will enable us to relate to him as our 'Abba' father, as our 'Mighty God', as our 'I Am that I Am' as our 'Desire of all Nations' etc.

Each of His other names such as Jehovah Sabaoth, Jehovah Shammah, Jehovah Tsidikenu, Jehovah Rohi, etc. is clearly explained and each reveals his character to us as His children.

The name of the Lord is a strong tower; the Righteous runneth into it and is safe. O Lord our Lord, how majestic is your name in all the earth! As we uplift and worship our God by calling upon His name, we will each begin to fly into an awesome level of experience like never before. This book is a must read for all who want to know God and experience his Divine attributes revealed in His Name.

Robert A. Kwarteng

INTRODUCTION

This book is intended to make the believer aware of the powerful tool that they possess in the names of the God that they serve and how to use them to their huge benefit.

A name is the principal manner in which a power, authority, person, creature, place, or object is identified or known. The name of a person, object or a place, frequently gives a clue about their nature, not least their character.

The Hebrew Old Testament names of God inform us of the nature of God's character. Having a clear knowledge and understanding of the names of God will greatly reward a believer. Knowing the names and attributes of God and using them appropriately enables you to give Him the reverence that He deserves.

The names of God can be categorized under two headings: The single Names of God and The Combination Names of God.

It must be made clear that the Names of God can also be found in singular or plural forms and there are times when these forms are combined or alternated in their use. The combination and alternations between singular form and plural form for the name of deity gives a strong credence to the Christian doctrine of the Trinity, which was always existent, but revealed fully in the New Testament. Christians have always believed in the Tri-unity (three-in-one, hence "Trinity") which is clearly taught in the Bible (the inspired Word of God).

CHAPTER ONE

THE SINGLE NAMES OF GOD

1. **EL** – "The Strong One".

This name is singular in form. El shows the character of strength and that God, El, is the first cause of all things, i.e. "...the most high God, the possessor of heaven and earth..." Genesis 14:22.

The title is often connected with such Divine characters as:

"Almighty God" – Genesis 17:1. In this scripture God reveals Himself to Abram as the most powerful God. He is the ultimate authority, there is none after Him and therefore Abram should take His word and instruction as final.

"Everlasting God" – Genesis 21:33. Abraham after having great encounters with God through the establishment, cutting and the fulfilment of the covenant (because Isaac had been born) had come to know and understand God as an everlasting God.

"The Living God" – Joshua 3:10. Joshua as the new leader of the Israelites was receiving messages directly from God as it happened to Moses. The truth of the matter is God was always acting according to his promises in these messages and so it was clear to Joshua that God is a living being who is able to interact with His people – hence he called the Israelites to come and listen to the words of the Living God. This description of God was the most appropriate, considering the fact that the gods of the surrounding nations like Canaanites, Hittites, Hivites, Perizzites, Girgashites, Amorites and Jebusites, showed no signs of life (Psalm 115).

"A Faithful God" – Deuteronomy 7:9. In this verse Moses reminded the Israelites of God's love for them and that He is a covenant keeper and would keep the oath that He had sworn since the time of their fathers.

2. ELOAH – "The Mighty One".

Also a singular title, this name comes from **AHLAH**, meaning to worship or to adore. This presents God as the one supreme object of worship. "...Thou art a God ready to pardon, gracious and merciful..." Nehemiah9:17. Nehemiah talked and wrote about the greatness of God by referring to the ingratitude and disobedience of the Israelites who had failed to worship God for the great things that He had done in the past for them, not least their deliverance from the hands of the Egyptians. The Bible, the inspired Word of God, indicates the Lord's complete control over human life and nature, hence He is rightly described as "Eloah", the Mighty One.

3. ELOHIM – "The Almighty".

ELOHIM is the plural form of ELOAH. It is used in Genesis 1:1, "...God created the heavens and the earth". It is used with the pronoun, "us"(plural) and "image" (singular) in Genesis 1:26, "Let us make man in our image", giving an early indication of the mystery of the "Tri-unity" of the Godhead.

4. JEHOVAH "HE IS" – "the self-Existing One".

This name is generally translated as "the LORD". The spelling was formed by inserting vowels to the Hebrew form YHWH to Yahweh. It is used in connection with Elohim in Genesis 2:4, "The LORD God (Jehovah Elohim) made..."

In the name, Jehovah, three periods of existence come together in one word: the past, the present, and the future – He that always was, that always is, and that ever is to come as is interpreted in Revelation 1:4. This name parallels "Lord" as used of Jesus Christ in the New Testament.

5. ADON – "Lord".

This is a singular form meaning Lord, Master, Possessor, or Proprietor. In Exodus 23:17, God is described as "Adon Jehovah".

6. ADONAHY – "Lord".

This is the plural form of ADON. It means "Lord" or "Master" in reference to a Divine title. This is the title Abram used for God in Genesis 15:2.

It is without doubt that these single names of God do show us who our God is, and why it is always a right decision to trust in Him. The chapters that follow will take us through the combination names of God which we use so frequently and yet might not understand fully. These chapters will inform, equip and empower us about how to use effectively the names of God to our benefit.

CHAPTER TWO

JEHOVAH ADONAHY (ADONAY)

This name is translated "God the Lord" of "the Lord God". This name of God means **JEHOVAH (IS) THE LORD.**

Psalm 68:20 declares, "He that is our God is the God of salvation; and unto GOD the Lord belong the issues from death". David overwhelmed by the greatness and the power of God, worships him by declaring that God is our deliverer and saviour, and it is He that determines our escape from death and difficult circumstances. He is the only one who sets us free from physical and eternal death. When considering the fact, that death is a powerful tool of destruction, if God is the only one that can save us from death, then there is no doubt about His sovereign power over our final destiny.

In Psalm 109:21; 140:7 and 141:8, David sings about the confidence that he has in God's protection for his life when he declared, "You have covered my head in the day of battle". All believers should learn from David's total trust in God and must express the same confidence in God's protective power over their life.

Habakkuk 3:19, declares, "The LORD God is my strength...". This is because the Hebrew people discovered that God was always on top of every situation they encountered and in *this* name of God the people of Israel found the power, bravery and authority to fight against their enemies, and also the guarantee of victory in all their wars, battles, challenges or troubles against their enemies. Let us remember that the nation of Israel being God's chosen people were always under attack from surrounding nations, who were serving other gods, but as they continually put their hope and trust in God they overcame these enemies, who seemed to command physical, numerical and military advantage over Israel. At no point in time, did the Israelites find God wanting when they obeyed Him and as a covenant keeping God, He always fulfils His promises. When the Israelites realised the extent of God's power and trustworthiness they saw God as their strength and hope, hence the name Jehovah Adonahy "Jehovah (is) the Lord". Believers, confessing this name, time and time again, will put God in the driver's seat (of their lives) as the Hebrews did and found relief and joy. Declaring that God is the LORD means that you have surrendered everything in your life to Him; He is in control and all you have to do is to call upon Him in time of need and He will answer you. As indeed it is declared that anyone who calls upon the name of the LORD shall be saved. There is power in the name of God – Psalm 18:3.

Activate the power in this name of God over your life by making the following declaration now and as often as you like:

Oh my soul (say your name in full), Jehovah Adonahy is the Lord of my salvation, Jehovah Adonahy is the Lord of my health, Jehovah Adonahy is the Lord of my finances, Jehovah Adonahy is the Lord of my whole life and destiny. Therefore I put my full trust and hope in Him and it shall be well with me. Amen

CHAPTER THREE

JEHOVAH ELOHIM

This name translates as "The LORD God" and this means **JEHOVAH IS GOD.**

This name could also be translated literally as Jehovah (the Self-Existing One), Elohim (The Almighty) – The Self-Existing Almighty One or The Self-Existing One and Almighty.

Since the creation of the heavens and the earth there has never been a shred of doubt amongst believers that they belong to a God whose awesome power manifests the fact that He is Self-Exi sting and Almighty. This is because in Genesis: chapters one and two where God's creative power is described in a lot of detail; we see the display of God's awesome and sovereign power and unquestionable authority. He called things that did not exist to come into being in an instant. Such is the great power and unsearchable wisdom of our God that His subjects have described Him as Jehovah Elohim "The LORD God" which means JEHOVAH IS GOD.

This name is a testimony to the fact that God has always been in complete control of the creation and the sustenance of the heavens and earth. Whatever God has considered an indispensable requirement for creation, He has provided out of His own power and authority, which is a clear indication of His Self-Existing and Almighty status.

Nothing can limit God and He is not accountable to anyone. This is why in Genesis chapter three, where the temptation by the serpent (satan) and fall of man is recorded, we see Adam and Eve trying to hide themselves and also cover themselves because of their sin, when they sensed the presence of the LORD God after their fall. They realised they had disobeyed an extraordinary living being that must not be disobeyed because of His unlimited and awesome power The Self-Existing and Almighty God. This was further corroborated by the fact that when God pronounced judgment upon Adam, Eve and the serpent, in His capacity as Jehovah Elohim, it was established straightaway.

In 2 Samuel 7:22, David in praising God said "wherefore thou art great, O LORD God: for there is none like thee, neither is there any God beside thee...". In effect David was saying God's sovereign nature, power and authority makes Him incomparable. His declaration "O LORD God" was a clear reference to His "Self-Existing" and "Almighty" status. David made this declaration after God had spoken through the prophet Nathan that He was going to establish David's kingdom forever (Christ's kingdom is forever established as God promised; His earthly descent and lineage is traced through David). David believed it because he had experienced the unstoppable power of God, work for him and Israel, and he therefore called God Jehovah Elohim "Self-Existing" and "Almighty" God.

Hezekiah in praying and asking the Lord for deliverance from his enemy Sennacherib declared in 2 Kings 19:19

"Save thou us out of his hand that all the kingdoms of the earth may know that thou art the LORD God, even thou only". Again the incomparable nature of God is expressed in Jehovah Elohim "Self-Existing" and "Almighty" God. This was to say that only a "Self-Existing" and "Almighty" God who is without any restriction on His power could deliver Hezekiah from a powerful enemy in Sennacherib. The same expressions about God are found in 1 Chronicles 17:16; 1 Chronicles 22:1; Psalm 72:18; Jonah 4:6; Genesis 2:4; Genesis 3:9; 2 Samuel 7:22; 2 Kings 19:19.

So as believers in the Lord Jesus Christ, we should feel secure in the knowledge that the God that we serve is Jehovah Elohim "The Self-Existing and Almighty One". We should rest assured that such a God is in total control of our lives and everything around us. So instead of murmuring about the challenges that we face each day in our lives we ought to go before our Jehovah Elohim in deep prayer asking in the name of Jesus and we shall receive (John 16:23-24). Murmuring is a sign of being spiritually weak and out of touch with Jehovah Elohim, our God who has no restriction in His power and ability to transform any situation that is in the heavens or on the earth. Let us be like the men and women of faith like Abraham, Moses, Jacob, Anna, Hannah and others who put their full trust in the LORD God who is "Self-Existing" and "Almighty" and were never disappointed because they trusted in Jehovah Elohim.

Activate the power in this name of God over your life by making the following declaration now and as often as you like:

Oh my soul (say your full name), I believe, as from today, that the LORD God that I serve is JEHOVAH ELOHIM and that there is no restriction on His power and authority in heaven and on earth, for He is Self-Existing and Almighty God. Therefore I claim and receive (mention your needs) from JEHOVAH ELOHIM to transform my life in Jesus' name. Amen.

CHAPTER FOUR

JEHOVAH SABAOTH (TSEBAOTH)

This name translates "The LORD of Hosts", which means **JEHOVAH OF THE (HEAVENLY) ARMIES.**

This is one of the magnificent names of God due to the importance of the roles that armies play in the lives of people. National armies honour important responsibilities not least the protection of their respective countries from outside aggression and also to attack enemy countries in times of war. In peace time, armies, among other institutions, are used to help in national development (for example used in building schools, roads and bridge construction), and in emergencies such as floods, earthquake and volcanic eruptions. Therefore, taken in the spiritual context, for the believer, it is a name of hope because it guarantees victory against all your enemies and the obstacles that you may face in your life. This name, which is translated "The LORD of Hosts" means Jehovah of the Heavenly armies. This is to say that the covenant keeping God is in total control of the magnificent and powerful heavenly armies or spiritual forces. It must also be made known that in addition; God is in total control of all terrestrial hosts (armies) or forces as well. In short God is in control of celestial (angelic) and terrestrial (human) hosts, armies or forces. This is obvious as He is the creator

THE POWER IN THE NAMES OF GOD

of heaven and earth, and all that is within it. What a hope and assurance for the believer, and the believer who knows this, grows in confidence of the LORD.

David gives us a clear example of what the name JEHOVAH SABAOTH means for the believer. As a young and innocent teenager, David appeared to have signed his own death warrant when he went into battle singlehandedly on behalf of Israel against an experienced, fearsome and powerful giant and warrior called Goliath (remember he had terrorised the armies of Israel, the people of God, for a number of days). However, since David knew the God that he had trusted in, when the Philistine cursed him by his gods, David simply replied, "This day will the LORD deliver thee into mine hand...for the battle is the LORD'S, and he will give you into our hands" (1 Samuel 17:43-47). Jehovah Sabaoth "Jehovah of the heavenly armies" responded and by the power of the throw of a single stone on to the forehead of Goliath, David won. At that moment the armies of heaven had taken over the battle following the instructions of their Commander-in-Chief, Jehovah Sabaoth and dealt efficiently with the enemy of God's people.

From the time of their exodus from Egypt to the time of the conquest and subsequent settlement of the land of Canaan, Jehovah Sabaoth who is **Jehovah of the heavenly armies** led, fought and won every battle for Israel against their enemies, as long as Israel lived in obedience to God. The nation of Israel was, for most of the time, surrounded by enemy nations who had numerical advantage over them but in battle after battle and war after war against these ungodly enemy nations,

Israel always won, as long as they obeyed God. For us, believers, this is our assurance of victory over satan, his agents and every single battle or war that we face or would face in our lives, because **JEHOVAH SABAOTH** has his armies ready to fight on our behalf. The armies of Jehovah Sabaoth do not fail or lose a battle. Victory is always a guarantee because no army in the spiritual or physical realm can stand against them.

During His arrest in the garden of Gethsemane, Peter out of fear and also zeal to protect Jesus, struck and cut off the ear of one of the people that belonged to the mob that had come to arrest Jesus. Jesus however rebuked Peter by asking him if he thought, he Jesus could not pray to His Father in heaven, asking Him to send more than twelve legions (72,000) of angels to come and fight for Him? A clear indication that our God has a mighty army at His disposal to fight on our behalf at any time that we need help. Glory be to God!

As a believer, the LORD of Hosts will fight every single battle in your life for you if you surrender your whole life and live in total obedience to Him. Indeed it is declared in Isaiah 31:1-5 that the Lord warns against His children who have put their faith in Egypt (the world) and evil systems to deliver them in times of need. The Lord assures His people by declaring, "....so shall the LORD of hosts come down to fight for mount Zion and for the hill thereof". Mount Zion stands for God's chosen people, Israel. Today God's chosen people for His Kingdom is the church, those who have been saved by the blood of Jesus. As believers we have nothing to fear, because the God that we serve is Jehovah of the heavenly armies. All our battles in the spiritual and physical realm and indeed in

THE POWER IN THE NAMES OF GOD

any area of our life must be surrendered unto Him. In fact the scriptures in Matthew 11:28 could not have been more emphatic when Jesus declared, "Come unto me all ye that labour and are heavy laden, and I will give you rest", and also in 1 Peter 5:7, "Casting all your care upon him; for he careth for you". The believer should stop murmuring and call upon Jehovah Sabaoth in faith and He will cause all their enemies to be defeated for them.

Activate the power in this name of God over your life by making the following declaration now and as often as you like:

Oh my soul (say your full name), I call upon the name of Jehovah Sabaoth, the LORD of Hosts, Jehovah of the heavenly armies to fight my battles for me. All my spiritual, health, financial, physical, emotional, psychological, physiological, moral battles and indeed every other battle in any area of my life, I surrender unto Jehovah Sabaoth and ask that He uses His heavenly armies on my behalf, and I believe my victory is guaranteed, as I claim it in Jesus' name. Amen.

God is also known as:

JEHOVAH ELOHE SABAOTH which is translated as "The LORD God of Hosts" means **JEHOVAH IS GOD OF THE (HEAVENLY) ARMIES** – 2 Samuel 5:10; 1 Kings 19:10; Psalm 59:5 and Psalm89:8.

ADONAHY (ADONAY) JEHOVAH SABAOTH (TSEBAOTH) which is translated as "The Lord, the LORD of Hosts" means **THE LORD, JEHOVAH OF THE (HEAVENLY) ARMIES** – Isaiah 1:24; Isaiah 10:16,33 and Isaiah 19:4.

ELOHIM SABAOTH (TSEBAOTH) – This is translated as "God of Hosts" which means **GOD OF THE (HEAVENLY) ARMIES** – Psalm 80:7,14.

JEHOVAH M'KADDESH – This is translated as "The Lord Who Sanctifies" – Leviticus 20:7-8.

JEHOVAH SHAMMAH – This is translated as "The Lord is There" – Ezekiel 48:35.

CHAPTER FIVE

ADONAHY JEHOVAH

This name is translated as "Lord God" and it means **THE LORD (IS) JEHOVAH** – Genesis 15:1-6; Deuteronomy 3:24; Psalm 73:28; Joshua 7:7; Judges 6:22 and Judges 16:28.

This name of God appears to be complementary to Jehovah Adonahy but it is not exactly so because it expresses a unique characteristic of God in His relationship with His people.

In Genesis 15:1-6 God made a clear promise to Abram (later called Abraham) by appearing to him in a vision and giving him a firm assurance that Abram should not be afraid even though he was childless at the time, and both he and his wife Sarai (later called Sarah) were very much advanced in age and appeared to have missed out on, reproducing their own biological child, that He would give him a lot of descendants, making them into a great nation. God declared unto him, "I am thy shield and exceeding great reward". Abram acknowledged the greatness of God by petitioning, "Lord GOD, what will you give me, seeing I go childless..." In other words Abram was saying "The Lord who is, who was, and who will always be in charge of my life and everything around me what can I gain from you since the promise about a large number of descendants in the covenant has still not been fulfilled".

The most significant thing about Abram's response is that he believed in God's sovereign power as Jehovah, which was attributed to him as righteousness. He never murmured against God. Believers should act according to how Abram showed his faith in God, and believe that His sovereign power will surely manifest itself in our anxious and difficult moments. We only have to ask without doubting and murmuring, because that is what Abram did and he received his exceeding great reward from God.

Activate the power in this name of God over your life by making the following declaration now and as often as you like:

Oh my soul (say your full name), today I declare the sovereign power of Jehovah to manifest in my life to give me my breakthrough and victory over every challenge that I face now and in the future, in Jesus' name. Amen.

CHAPTER SIX

EL ELYON (HEBREW) OR
ELAHA ILLAYA (ARAMAIC)

This name of God is translated "The most high God", or "the High God". This means **GOD (IS) THE HIGH ONE.**

This name of God rightly describes Him and also explains His position in relation to His creation.

In welcoming Abram from his pursuit and victory over the captors of Abram's nephew Lot, Melchizedek, king of Salem, blessed him, and said, "Blessed be Abram of the most high God, possessor of heaven and earth. And blessed be the Most High God which hath delivered thine enemies into thine hand" (Genesis 14:19-20).

The battle that Abram went into was a very difficult one and by human account, it was an impossible feat for Abram to achieve. This is because Abram had to deliver Lot, his brother's son who had been caught in a battle between two alliances of kings. Lot was part of the plunder that Cherdorlaomer's alliance took from Sodom and Gomorrah after their victory over Bera's alliance. When Abram heard the news, he made the effort to go and rescue Lot from his captors. According to Genesis 14:14-16, with only three hundred and eighteen trained servants, Abram was able to pursue and defeat a powerful alliance of four kings who were intimidating and destroying rival alliances. This was only possible because Abram served the most high God, possessor of heaven and earth, whilst the alliance of the four kings and their nations served other gods that had no life in them. These lifeless gods were like those described in Psalm 115, "...They have mouths, but they speak not: eyes have they, but they see not: They have ears, but they hear not: noses have they, but they smell not: They have hands, but they handle not: feet have they, but they walk not: neither speak they through their throat. They that make them are like unto them; so is every one that trusteth in them".

The power of El Elyon "the most High God" overwhelmed Nebuchadnezzar when he tried to substitute God with himself by making a decree that everybody in the Babylonian kingdom should worship his huge image or statue made of gold. However he got the shock of his life when he was openly defied by three Jews, Shadrach (Hananiah), Meshach (Mishael) and Abednego (Azariah) who were servants of the most high God. In his anger Nebuchadnezzar instructed for them to be cast into a burning fiery furnace, but what followed afterwards was simply unbelievable. Nebuchadnezzar and his nobles saw these three men who had been thrown into the overheated burning furnace bound hands and feet, set loose and walking in the fire with no hurt, and in their company was a fourth person whom Nebuchadnezzar himself testified that looked like the Son of God. He saw the overwhelming power of God work against him but in favour of Shadrach, Meshach and Abednego. Realising that his action against the three men had no effect, he gave up and asked them to come out of the fire. He had accepted the fact that he was fighting a losing battle against an almighty God who was full of power and could do anything, anytime and anywhere. By his own admission, he called the three men, "...ye servants of the most High God".

As a believer you may be going through a very difficult situation, which may even pose a challenge to compromise your faith and surrender to the godless principles and systems of this world. Principles and systems that look intimidating, convincing and acceptable in many ways but are evil, false, temporary and unreliable. They cannot match the power of God which works in perfection in the heavens and on the earth, and in our lives. Just as Nebuchadnezzar gave up on Shadrach, Meshach and Abednego because he saw the awesome power of God working against him, but in favour of His (God's) servants, even so, will satan and his agents give up on you, when they see the power and the favour of God work on your behalf, as the Lord's compassions are made new for you, every day of your life.

As a believer let your faith in God continue to grow because He is "El Elyon", "the most High God" or "The High One". Serving the most High God means you are a privileged soul. In times of challenges or difficulties remember that the most High God is able to deliver you since He holds the whole heavens, the earth, and everything within it under His mighty control.

Activate the power in this name of God over your life by making the following declaration now and as often as you like:

Oh my soul (say your full name) know that the God that I serve is El Elyon, the most High God, who is able to provide for me, protect me, heal me and deliver me from any difficult circumstances. There is therefore nothing for me to be afraid of, since He is in control of everything in heaven, on earth and around me.

CHAPTER SEVEN

EL ROI

This name of God is translated "God seest me". This means **GOD (IS) THE ONE WHO SEES ME.** Genesis 16:7-16.

This name of God assures or gives the believer comfort in their moments of trial and afflictions. Hagar, Sarai's maid, had a problem with her mistress after she had conceived a child for Abram (Sarai's husband). After being severely disciplined by Sarai, she fled and went into the wilderness. Whilst in the wilderness and being alone, she felt rejected and was full of fear, but the angel of the LORD appeared unto her to return and submit herself to Sarai. The angel of the LORD then spoke words of comfort and gave her the assurance that he will multiply her seed exceedingly, through her son Ishmael, who was to be born to her. Having received this favour from the LORD, Hagar's relief, joy and comfort led her to call God "El Roi", "Thou God seest me". Hagar did not think that she was recognisable enough for God to take notice of her problem and come to her aid. This is the problem that many believers experience today. When they are faced with challenges, trials and afflictions, they tend to think that their cries for help do not reach God and that God does not take any notice of them, but this is wrong. For God who is Omnipotent, Omniscient and Omnipresent sees and knows every single believer and all His creation in every situation and He will surely respond to your cries for help as He has declared in Isaiah 49:14-16, "But Zion said, The LORD has forsaken me, and my Lord hath forgotten me. Can a woman forget her sucking child, that she should not have compassion on the son of her womb? Yea, they may forget, yet will I not forget thee. Behold, I have graven thee upon the palms of my hands; thy walls are continually before me". So you see, you do count before God, as being graven upon the palms of God's hands means that you will always receive His attention. Never give up on your faith in God no matter what you are going through, because you count in God's plan and He will never forsake you. Hagar experienced it, Israel experienced it, many believers have experienced it, I have experienced it and so shall you experience it as you look up to God.

Activate the power in this name of God over your life by making the following declaration now and as often as you like:

Oh my soul (say your name), the God that I serve is a God that sees me in every situation that I find myself in, and He shall surely meet me at the point of my need.

CHAPTER EIGHT

EL SHADDAY (SHADDAI)

This name of God is translated "Almighty God", "God Almighty" or "The Almighty". El Shadday (Shaddai) means GOD (IS) THE ALL-POWERFUL ONE – Genesis 17:4; Genesis 43:14 and Job 8:5.

This name is one of the most commonly used, by present day believers of God. By using this name often for God, believers rightly acknowledge that God is indeed Almighty, all-powerful and all-conquering.

God's almighty and all-powerful nature is seen in His creative power from the beginning of the universe and His redemptive power through Jesus Christ. In creation, God is the sovereign creator of matter, energy, space and time. In addition, to being the sovereign creator, He is the sustainer of everything both seen and unseen. No other power can compare to God's "Almighty" and "All-powerful" position. After the fall and separation of man from God, man's fellowship with God was broken. There was, therefore, the need of redemption of man, from eternal condemnation, and God through Christ has provided it. In the birth, death and resurrection of Jesus which is the hope of the believer's salvation, the "Almighty" and "All-powerful" nature of God is seen at work. Believers should gain confidence in the fact that

God's "Almighty" and "All-powerful" status guarantees us hope in this present time and as well as the future.

The "Almighty" nature of God is seen in His dealings with His people and the world. He has always had the power to create and control everything in the heavens, on the earth and below the earth. A few examples from the Bible illustrate this belief:

Noah's deliverance from the flood.

The birth of Isaac to Abraham and Sarah.

Joseph's sale into slavery and elevation in Egypt.

His mighty deliverance of Israel from Egypt.

David's defeat of Goliath and the Philistines.

The birth and work of John the Baptist.

The birth, death and resurrection of Jesus Christ.

The Holy Spirit's baptism of the apostles.

The birth and growth of the church.

Consider your past life before you were saved by Jesus.

These examples are just the tip of the iceberg of the "Almighty" nature of God. As a believer your faith, hope and joy in the Lord must increase as you recall His mighty acts in your life. Call upon your God as El Shadday in every second, of your life, because with Him in control of your life you are certainly an "over comer". The miracles of Christ, as recorded in the Bible, clearly demonstrate the "Almighty" power of God at work. In His earthly ministry, all powers, both spiritual and natural, surrendered to the "Almighty" power of Jesus

Christ (God, the Son). Remember that at the mention of His name, every knee bows and every tongue confesses that Jesus Christ is Lord, to the glory of God, the Father. There is no power that can resist the "Almighty" power of God in the name of Jesus.

Every believer must count themselves as blessed and privileged to be children of El Shaddai, "the Almighty God" and "The All-powerful One". That is why Paul said in Romans 8:31, "...If God be for us, who can be against us?"

Activate the power in this name of God over your life by making the following declaration now and as often as you like:

Oh my soul (say your name), I rejoice for I serve El Shaddai, who is the Almighty God and the All – powerful One, and therefore who can be against me?

CHAPTER NINE

EL OLAM

This name of God is translated as "The Everlasting God" and it means GOD (IS) THE ETERNAL ONE.

Genesis 21:33, Deuteronomy 33:27, Psalm 146:10, Psalm 90:2, Psalm 93 and Revelation 1:8.

This name of God clearly reveals one of God's most fundamental attributes; everlasting or eternal existence. That God has always been and will always be in existence (eternity) has never been a problem for the believer. The holy Bible, which is the word of God, is replete with this belief that God is "The Everlasting God" or "The Eternal God". The opening sentence of the Bible in Genesis 1:1 reads: "In the beginning God created the heaven and the earth", which is to say that the pre-existing, everlasting and eternal God created the heaven and the earth.

The deity and the eternity of Christ is revealed in John 1:1 "In the beginning was the Word, and the Word was with God, and the Word was God". In Revelation 1:8 Christ speaks to John and says, "I am Alpha and Omega, the beginning and the ending, saith the Lord, which is, and which was, and which is to come, the Almighty". This scripture clearly indicates the eternal nature of Jesus

Christ, the Son of God, and hence the eternal and everlasting nature of God, the Father. Psalm 93, which describes and explains the majesty of God also declares of God, "Thy throne is established of old: thou art from everlasting".

Moses, in blessing the children of Israel before his death, declared in Deuteronomy 33:27 "The eternal God is thy refuge, and underneath are the everlasting arms: and He shall thrust out the enemy from before thee; and shall say, Destroy them". Moses, a man to whom God had made many appearances and also spoken to by word of mouth, in his last days upon the face of this earth acknowledged God's greatness and eternity. That is why, in his parting message, he assured the Israelites that the Eternal God is their refuge, and that He shall throw out their enemies from before them. Certainly there could never have been a greater testimony and words of assurance given by Moses to the people of Israel concerning God. Moses, having had numerous encounters with God, was the best placed person to give any testimony concerning God. Therefore, for him to declare God, as Eternal or Everlasting, "El Olam" is surely nothing but pure truth about the nature of God. Moses assured the children of Israel that the Eternal God will always be there to protect them, fight their battles for them and destroy their enemies. This is because those enemies of Israel all served idols, who were dead, temporal and powerless.

Beloved, to serve our God who is ETERNAL or EVERLASTING means we are worshipping a true and living God who neither sleeps nor slumbers and protects and guides us every day. Just as the Israel of the Old

Testament benefitted from the power of El Olam, "The Everlasting God", even so, is the Israel of The New Testament (the Church) benefitting from this same God as well.

As a believer, your greatest hope is this, that the God that you serve is "The Eternal One", "The Everlasting God". Your faith is therefore a living faith, and your hope a living hope. This is because your God is alive and alive forever more. This is the greatest privilege anyone can have in life. That our God is El Olam also means that He is definitely coming back to judge the living and the dead. Therefore, as believers, we must prepare ourselves and be ready for the glorious second coming of our Lord and saviour, Jesus Christ.

Activate the power in this name of God over your life by making the following declaration now and as often as you like:

Oh my soul (say your name) know that the Lord God that I serve is "El Olam", "God is the Eternal One". There is therefore hope in this God and I will continue to serve Him always that it may be well with me.

CHAPTER TEN

EL GIBBOR

This name of God is translated "The mighty God", which also means "GOD IS THE WARRIOR" – Isaiah 9:6; Isaiah 10:21 and Exodus 17:16.

In this name, there is assurance for the people of God that He is full of power, authority and the ability to deliver His people from any form of attack or bondage in both the spiritual and physical realm. There is no doubt about the fact that, attacks and bondages are common occurrences in a believer's life; hence the knowledge and understanding that a powerful God with the characteristics of a mighty warrior, who is able to deliver us, exists, is very reassuring.

Isaiah 9:6 reads, "for unto us a child is born, unto us a son is given: and the government shall be upon his shoulder: and his name shall be called Wonderful, Counsellor, The Mighty God, The Everlasting Father, The Prince of Peace". This verse of scripture is part of a prophecy about the birth of Jesus Christ the Messiah. In this prophecy, God promises to set His people free, through His mighty deliverance. His people, Israel, who were living in spiritual darkness and under oppression and suppression of satan and sin, needed salvation.

Therefore the nature of the Messiah, who was to come and execute this deliverance of Israel from their oppressive and suppressive captivity, was revealed in the prophecy in Isaiah 9:6. Among the names by which He was to be known, was "The Mighty God" who fights like a great warrior. The world needs a spiritual warrior to deliver it from spiritual attack and bondage. Battles call for

warriors. Jesus Christ, who is described as The Mighty God and leads us in our battles against satan, satan's agents, and all sorts of demonic entities, is our Mighty Warrior, as He continues to bring us victory upon victory against the world of evil and darkness.

In a remarkable experience in Exodus 17:8-16, the LORD leads His nation Israel into a battle with Amalek, the bitter enemies of Israel. Amalek was defeated and the LORD being the true Mighty Warrior declared that He will utterly put out the remembrance of Amalek from under heaven. This is one of the many instances whereby the LORD led His people into battle, fought and won the battles for them. Let us remember that He has armies at His disposal.

As a believer of Jesus Christ and the child of God, you have to begin to let it sink into your spirit that you have nothing to fear so long as you live in obedience to the LORD. This is because our LORD and GOD is a Mighty Warrior who will fight and win every single battle in our lives. It doesn't matter what kind of battle it is. Be it spiritual, physical, psychological, financial or medical, our GOD who is the Mighty Warrior, will fight and win for us, so cheer up always.

Activate the power in this name of God over your life by making the following declaration now and as often as you like:

Oh my soul (say your name), fear not but rejoice because the LORD my GOD is "THE WARRIOR" who will fight and win every battle for me.

CHAPTER ELEVEN

EL CHAI (HAI)

This name of God translates as "The living God".

Joshua 3:10; Revelation 1:18-19; Exodus 3:1-8 and Deuteronomy 5:26.

When God miraculously appeared to Moses near the mountain of God in Horeb, He spoke to Moses and Moses replied Him. He then called Moses to leadership, for the deliverance of His people from slavery in Egypt. What happened between God and Moses is very clear, two living beings interacting; one of the beings is supreme and invisible, the other subordinate and visible. This was the first evidence to Moses that the power that spoke to him was a living being. Further evidence followed in the form of the signs and wonders that God displayed; the staff of Moses turning into a snake and vice versa, his hand turning leprous and then being restored, the encounters with Pharaoh's magicians, the ten plagues in Egypt and many more, as recorded in the book of Exodus and some of the other books written by Moses.

On the few occasions that God spoke unto the whole assembly of Israel, out of the midst of the fire, out of the cloud, or out of the thick darkness with a great voice, they were terrified of the power, the glory and the greatness of the living God. In Exodus 5:24 the word of God says "And ye said, Behold, the LORD our God hath shewed us his glory and his greatness, and we have heard his voice out of the midst of the fire: we have seen this day that God doth talk with man, and he liveth". Again in Exodus 5:26 the people of Israel confessed, "For who is there of all flesh, that have heard the voice of the living God speaking out of the midst of the fire, as we have, and lived?" In other words, despite, the terrifying experience of hearing the voice of God directly, it still pleased the Israelites, in that it gave them the confidence that the God that they serve, is an awesome living God, who is on their side because He has not and will not destroy them.

Child of God and servant of Christ you need to exercise this faith that the God that you serve is a living God. He speaks unto you and affects your life on a daily basis; He guides, protects and provides for you every day of your life. This is a blessed assurance for every believer in Christ. Experiencing the living God brings you victory in every challenge that you face in your life; as the Israelites discovered in Joshua 3:10, "And Joshua said, Hereby ye shall know that the living God is among you, and that without fail, drive out from before you the Canaanites, and the Hittites, and the Hivites, and the Perizzites, and the Girgashites, and the Amorites, and the Jebusites". Only a living God can make life worth living for you and Christ, as our living saviour, is doing just that. In the book of Revelation 1:18, Jesus declared to Apostle John, "I am he that liveth, and was dead; and behold, I am alive for evermore, Amen; and have the keys of hell and death". What a declaration? Our God is a living God!

Activate the power in this name of God over your life by making the following declaration now and as often as you like:

Oh my soul (say your name), be full of joy and assurance because the God that I serve is a living God who knows me, and can hear and answer me when I call upon him. I continue to trust in him for he is my shield and buckler.

CHAPTER TWELVE

EL KANNA

This name of God translates as "The Jealous God".

Exodus 20:1-5; Deuteronomy 4:24 and John 2:13-17.

From the day of creation up until now God has always wanted an exclusive relationship between Himself and the human race. This is exemplified by His relationship with Adam and Eve, Abraham, Isaac, Jacob (Israel) and many other individuals in the Bible. This is rightly so because upon creating the heavens and the earth and everything within it, he created us, humans, in His own image. Creating us, in His own image, means that God has great love for us. There is also further proof of His special love for us, by the sacrifice of His only begotten son, Jesus Christ, for our sins. Therefore, God wants us for Himself only. He is not prepared to share our allegiance to Him with anybody.

In Exodus 20:1-5, as part of the Ten Commandments that God gave His people Israel, He reminded them of how He had rescued them from their slavery in Egypt and therefore made it explicitly clear to them that they must not trust in and worship any other gods apart from Him. It must be noted that God's relationship with His people can be interpreted in many ways, including;

King-subject, master-servant, creator-created (potter-clay), and husband-wife. All these relationships portray a close bond between the two parties. The close bond of affection ranges from emotional to spiritual intimacy between God and the human race, most especially, believers in Christ Jesus. Anybody who has worked so hard to establish a relationship with another person would not be prepared to see it break down or get destroyed. They would take effective action to protect the relationship.

Therefore if our God is a jealous God, He is so on the basis of divine jealousy so that we would not lose our way and become spiritual harlots (like the Israel of old did many times by breaking the covenant between God and themselves). That is why Apostle Paul wrote in 2 Corinthians 11:2, "For I am jealous over you with godly jealousy: for I have espoused you to one husband that I may present you as a chaste virgin to Christ". As believers in Christ Jesus, we are to serve Him only, and with a great amount of zeal. We should not dilute or strain the relationship between Christ and ourselves by offering our worship to any other powers, idols, graven images or activities or things. Pleasures and attractions of the flesh can consume so much of our time and shift our focus from Christ. If we are not careful, we will devote most of our time for social activities like parties, watching television, and seeking our selfish financial interests like doing overtime hours of work to the detriment of our serious participation in events concerning the kingdom of Christ. Before we become seriously aware, we have substituted God with these addictions in our life and this is very dangerous.

The moment we do this, we lose our blessings from God, because we become detached from Him. Just as a husband is jealous over his wife, even so, is God our maker and saviour, jealous over us with divine jealousy. Let us allow the zeal of the House of God to eat us up (John 2:17).

Activate the power in this name of God over your life by making the following declaration now and as often as you like:

Oh my soul (say your name), I know that the LORD my God is a jealous God. I therefore love the LORD my God with all my heart, and with all my soul and with my entire mind and He shall bless me.

Chapter Thirteen

EL HANNUN

This name of God translates as "The Merciful God".

Deuteronomy 4:29-31; John 8:1-11 and Psalm 103: 8-14.

It is the nature of God Almighty to be merciful to His people and creation; otherwise a world full of wickedness and ungodly acts would have been wiped out of existence by God long ago. Since the time of creation, God has always demonstrated great mercy or compassion towards humankind. It all began in the Garden of Eden where Adam and Eve, despite the Lord God's display of wonderful love and abundant provision for them, still managed to disobey God by allowing satan to deceive them. They fell spiritually and physically, lost their status in God's creation order, and, therefore, were expelled from the Garden of Eden. They lost their privileged position that God had given them in the order of creation. However God did not abandon nor destroy them. Being a merciful God, He still provided for them when they were lacking in material provision, as is declared in Genesis 3:21, "Unto Adam also and to his wife did the LORD God make coats of skins, and clothed them".

In Deuteronomy 4:29-31, as part of the summary of the covenant, God strongly warned the people of Israel against breaking the law, especially regarding worshipping other gods. Moses gave a detailed explanation with the help of examples about the consequences of following other gods. The punishment was that they would utterly perish from the land that the LORD God had given them as a possession and also that they would be scattered among the heathen. Moses, however, gave them the assurance that if they repented and turned to the LORD their God and became obedient unto His voice, the LORD their God is a merciful God and would not forsake them.

As a covenant keeping God, it was the merciful nature of God that caused Him to establish various covenants with His people in the Old Testament, which culminated in the sacrifice of His dear son Jesus Christ and the establishment of the New and everlasting covenant for all mankind. He is a merciful God.

Jesus, in His earthly ministry, always showed mercy to the people He met. In John 8:1-11, a woman who had been caught in adultery was brought to Jesus for condemnation and death by her accusers. The accusers were however shocked, when instead of condemning her to death in accordance with the Mosaic law, Jesus rather showed the woman great mercy and asked her to go and sin no more. This was after Jesus had challenged the woman's accusers to stone her, if they had not sinned before. Jesus' response to their own action, led them to see their own shortcomings and to realise that they lived at the mercy of God. Psalm 118, Psalm 136, Psalm 145:8-9 all tell us about the mercy of God.

Psalm 86:15 declares, "But thou, O Lord, art a God full of compassion, and gracious, longsuffering, and plenteous in mercy and truth". Also Psalm 145:8 declares,

"The LORD is gracious, and full of compassion; slow to anger and of great mercy". Psalm 136:1-26 then praises God for His mercy, which is seen in creation, the deliverance of His people from their enemies, and the provision of resources to meet the needs of His people.

As believers of our Lord and saviour Jesus Christ, we must appreciate the fact that every single breath of our life is filled with the Lord's mercy and love. Without the Lord's mercy there would have been no room for repentance and grace for any soul and we would all have been destined to a life of condemnation, as it is written in 1 Peter 1:3, "Blessed be the God and Father of our Lord Jesus Christ, which according to his abundant mercy hath begotten us again unto a lively hope by the resurrection of Jesus Christ from the dead".

We depend on the Lord's mercy every day for our lives and also our hope for the future. This is what the prophet, Jeremiah, confessed as part of his faith, when he said, "It is of the Lord's mercies that we are not consumed, because his compassion fails not. They are new every morning: great is thy faithfulness" (Lamentations 3:22-23). Without the Lord's mercy, compassion and love, life would have been impossible for us all, including the ignorant unbeliever. This is because the Lord's mercy is seen and felt in our salvation for eternal life, deliverance and protection from all forms of attack; our deliverance, his abundant provision for our needs, our decision making, our marriages and family lives, our working lives, our spiritual lives, and every area of our lives.

As children of God we are to remember that it is the mercy of God that sustains us day by day, for before we came to know Christ, many of us were murderers, sorcerers, witches, railers, thieves, fornicators, adulterers, rapists, etc, etc. Let us therefore develop the attitude of casting ourselves on to God's mercy every time, even as David declared in 2 Samuel 24:14, "I am in a great strait: let us fall now into the hand of the LORD; for his mercies are great: and let me not fall into the hand of man".

However let us not take undue advantage of the fact that because our God is full of mercy we should indulge ourselves in acts that will go against the principles of God and his kingdom. To do that, is wrong, as we are not only abusing God's mercy but also putting him to the test which is a serious sinful act with very serious consequences; for, "It is a fearful thing to fall into the hands of the living God" (Hebrews 10:31) and also, "For our God is a consuming fire" (Hebrews 12:29).

Nevertheless our God is merciful for, "The LORD is merciful and gracious, slow to anger, and plenteous in mercy. He will not always chide: neither will he keep his anger forever. He hath not dealt with us after our sins; nor rewarded us according to our iniquities. For as the heaven is high above the earth, so great is his mercy toward them that fear him. As far as the east is from the west, so far hath he removed our transgressions from us. Like as a father pitieth his children, so the LORD pitieth them that fear him. For he knoweth our frame; he remembereth that we are dust" (Psalm 103:8-14).

Activate the power in this name of God over your life by making the following declaration now and as often as you like:

Oh my soul (say your name), this day know that the LORD my God is a merciful God. I will therefore be obedient to Him and enjoy His mercy forever more.

CHAPTER FOURTEEN

EL AVRAHAM, YITZAK V – YACOV

This name of God translates as "The God of Abraham, Isaac, and Jacob".

Exodus 3:15 and John 8:38-39.

When God miraculously appeared unto Moses at Horeb, the mountain of God, and called him to leadership, to deliver the Israelites out of Egypt, Moses wanted to know the identity of the mighty God he was dealing with. Among the descriptions that God gave of himself, he said, "Thus shalt thou say unto the children of Israel, the LORD God of your fathers, the God of Abraham, the God of Isaac, and the God of Jacob(Israel), hath sent me unto you: this is my name forever, and this is my memorial unto all generations" (Exodus 3:15).

God gave this identification of himself to the Israelites through Moses in order to remind them of his special relationship with these three faithful servants through whom, God, not only established the nation of Israel, but also established a covenant, constituting an important link in all that God began to do, has done throughout history, and will continue to do for his people until the consummation of history.

God had a special relationship with Abraham, Isaac and Jacob (Israel). This special relationship began with

Abraham, whom God called out of his kindred and led to a land, Abraham did not know. God then established a covenant with Abraham. In this covenant in Genesis 12:1-3, God made promises to Abraham in three areas: 1) National – "I will make of thee a great nation", 2) Personal – "I will bless thee, and make thy name great; and thou shall be a blessing", and 3) Universal – "In thee shall all families of the earth be blessed".

God's special relationship with Abraham was full of promises and the fulfilment of all promises. The fulfilment of these promises was proof of the fact that God was in control of Abraham's life, and this, also applies, to every child of God. We should therefore remain patient and wait upon the Lord, for He shall, surely, fulfil every promise that he has made, concerning our life, because his promises are yea and amen. The promise of the birth of Isaac, in particular, was challenging because Abraham was very concerned about having no child to be an heir to his wealth and property. So concerned was Abraham, to the point that, when God assured him in a vision, "I am thy shield, and thy exceeding great reward" (Genesis 15:1), Abram questioned God about his childless situation. It was his major concern because, not only, would he be without a natural heir to survive him after his death but there would be no descendants after him as well. However, when God assured him that his descendants would be as many as the stars of heaven, he believed in the LORD; and it was credited to him for righteousness – Genesis 15:6. Even after this assurance, the wait and the desperation, led Sarai to propose the carnal plan for children which led to Abram and Hagar giving birth to

Ishmael, but God still insisted that the promise of a child by Sarai was established and it would still be fulfilled. Sometimes, we, as children of God, can find situations too distressful and desperate that we overlook God's promises in His word to us and instead, take our own course of action, only to realize how unproductive our decisions and actions were. However as God's promises are always yea and amen, Isaac, the son of promise, was born to prove to Abraham and Sarah that nothing is too hard for the LORD, and that God was really his God.

God's relationship with Abraham was that of sure promises and belief. The same relationship still exists between God and us today as the spiritual descendants and heirs of Abraham. Abraham's wonderful relationship with God even deepened after a faith test in which God asked Abraham to sacrifice unto him Isaac (the son of promise). When Abraham willingly obeyed, he realized the ever-faithful and generous nature of the God that he served (God provided a ram in the place of Isaac for the sacrifice), hence he named the place of sacrifice Jehovah-jireh, meaning the LORD will provide. As a believer you need to know that the God of Abraham has not changed and that as spiritual heirs of Abraham, this relationship is our heritage to enjoy – God's promises in the new covenant established through his Son Jesus Christ.

Isaac is the testimony of the fulfilment of the covenant that God made between himself and Abraham. Being a testimony of this covenant meant that Isaac obviously enjoyed the provisions of the covenant as the LORD made it clear to him in Genesis 26:2-5, "And the LORD appeared unto him, and said, Go not down into Egypt; dwell in the land which I shall tell thee of: Sojourn in this land, and I will be with thee, and will bless thee; for unto thee, and unto thy seed, I will give all these countries, and I will perform the oath which I swore unto Abraham thy father; And I will make thy seed to multiply as the stars of heaven, and will give unto thy seed all these countries; and in thy seed shall all the nations of the earth be blessed; Because that Abraham obeyed my voice, and kept my charge, my commandments, my statutes, and my laws". All the provisions of the covenant God made with his father, Abraham, were confirmed to him and his descendants. They were blessed to the point that they became a great nation on the face of this earth. God made him a symbol of protection, provision, and prosperity.

Jacob, the grandson of Abraham, also tapped into the covenant that God had made with his grandfather, Abraham (Genesis 13:14-17; Genesis 15:1-7, 18- 21; Genesis 17:1-8). Jacob's favour from God began in the womb of his mother when God declared unto Rebekah that the twins in her womb were two nations but one of the nations shall be stronger than the other; and the elder (Esau) shall serve the younger (Jacob) – Genesis 25:22-23. This was confirmed when Esau foolishly sold his birthright by trading it to Jacob for a bowl of stew made from lentils (Genesis 25:29-34). This act led to Jacob gaining Esau's blessing from Isaac (Genesis chapter 27). On his escape from Esau to his ancestral homeland of Haran, he spent a night at Bethel where he dreamt about angels going up and down a ladder, and there received assurance of God's blessings (Genesis 28:1-19). The assurance that God gave him in the dream was a repeat and confirmation of the covenant that He (God) had made with Abraham and Isaac; an indication of the fact that as He has always been a faithful God to Abraham and Isaac, so will He be to Jacob, as well. In fact this promise was significantly enhanced for Jacob when, on his return journey from Haran, he wrestled with an angel at the river Jabbok and God changed his name to Israel (Genesis 32:22-32), a name that came with a new identity (he was now a prince of God and no longer a trickster), and tremendous blessings from God. Jacob's life was full of God's grace and blessings. His own uncle and father-in-law, Laban, testified of this (Genesis 30:27-43). Even as he travelled to Egypt with his family to escape a famine in Canaan, God spoke to him in a vision to assure him of his protection and blessing (Genesis 46:1-6).

Just as all these three patriarchs (Abraham, Isaac, and Jacob) were blessed immensely through God's covenant, with one man (Abraham), even so, will God Almighty, continue to bless every believer through the New Covenant that He has established, by His only begotten Son, Jesus. As you read this message be encouraged that the God of Abraham, Isaac, and Jacob is your God too and He will bless you and your descendants as He did for the patriarchs of Israel. Amen.

Activate the power in this name of God over your life by making the following declaration now and as often as you like:

Oh my soul (say your name), today the God of Abraham, Isaac, and Jacob has declared that He is my God too. Therefore the blessings of the covenant are mine too.

CHAPTER FIFTEEN

JEHOVAH NISSI

This name of God translates as "The Lord My Banner".
Exodus 17:15 and Hebrew 12:2.

A banner is a flag or other piece of cloth bearing a symbol, logo, slogan, or other message. It could be attached to a staff or two and used by a group of people in a procession or demonstration. In the past it could be used as a standard by a monarch, military commander, or knight in peace and war times. It could also be described as the flag of a nation, state or an army. These days, a banner could be used in a church with a scripture verse on it. It could even be used by a club with their motto on it as a form of identification. Hence a banner is a clear and powerful means by which a person or group of persons may choose to declare their identity whether in private or public.

Exodus 17:8-15 describes one of the remarkable victories won by Israel against their enemies. Their miraculous victory over the Amalekites was achieved when Moses went on top of a hill with the rod of God in his hand, ably assisted by Aaron and Hur. As long as his hands were held up, Israel's army, led by Joshua, was winning the battle but when he let down his hands

Israel, started losing. Therefore with the support of Aaron and Hur, Moses' heavy hands were kept up until the going down of the sun and Israel defeated the Amalekites.

This experience, of Israel against Amalek, is a strong indication of the fact that victory came to Israel as their leader, Moses, took along with him the rod of God which was a clear sign of their identification (their banner), in contrast to the Amalekites who did not worship the true God. Their victory only came, after Moses had continuously held up his hands, as he held the rod of God.

As a believer, your banner is the LORD Jesus Christ. With Jesus as your banner you are bound to face many difficulties in this world, simply because your face does not fit into the world's carnal system. When it happens to you, do not be discouraged, but rather be encouraged for the Lord has declared in John 15:18-20, "If the world hate you, ye know that it hated me before it hated you. If ye were of the world, the world would love his own: but because ye are not of the world, but I have chosen you out of the world, therefore the world hateth you. Remember the word that I said unto you, the servant is not greater than his lord. If they have persecuted me, they will persecute you; if they have kept my saying, they will keep yours also". However there is a reward for this as our Lord declares in Luke 6:22-23, "Blessed are ye, when men shall hate you, and when they shall separate you from their company, and shall reproach you, and cast out your name as evil, for the Son of man's sake. Rejoice ye in that day, and leap for joy: for, behold, your reward is great in heaven: for in the like manner did their fathers unto the prophets". There is surely an eternal reward and rejoicing in heaven for having Jesus as your banner.

Apostle Paul, realizing the power in using Jesus Christ as our banner, declared in Romans 1:16-17, "For I am not ashamed of the gospel of Christ: for it is the power of God unto salvation to everyone that believeth; to the Jew first, and also to the Greek. For therein is the righteousness of God revealed from faith to faith: as it is written, THE JUST SHALL LIVE BY FAITH". Thus a person can only be saved under this banner – the gospel of Christ.

Having Jesus Christ as our banner also enables us to overcome the world and all the evil attacks that come from it, 1 John 5:5 declares, "Who is he that overcometh the world, but he that believeth that Jesus is the Son of God?" We, as believers, therefore must continue to hold on to our faith, that Jesus is the Son of God and our saviour, and with Him, as our banner, we are always guaranteed our victory over satan, his agents and all the powers of darkness.

As believers we are most privileged to have a banner that: secures us eternal life, covers us, and guarantees us victory over our enemies, gives us a new identity, and gives us hope for the now and in eternity.

As a believer your greatest banner in your new life is the name of Jesus. In this name is your hope and destiny established. Let us lift up our banner (Jesus Christ) by proclaiming his name across all the nations through our full obedience and faithful service to Him. That way we secure our victory over the world, like the Israelites over the Amalekites when Moses lifted up their banner "the rod of God".

Activate the power in this name of God over your life by making the following declaration now and as often as you like:

Oh my soul (say your full name), I pick up and use my banner Jehovah Nissi, which is my identification so that I can overcome my enemies.

CHAPTER SIXTEEN

JEHOVAH ROPHI (RAPHA)

This name of God translates as "The Lord Who Heals You".

Exodus 15:26 and John 9:1-7.

Healing is one of the greatest needs of a person. It comes in various forms; physical, psychological, emotional, and spiritual. A lot of believers may at one point or the other need one or many forms of healing because of the complicated nature of life. When that happens we should automatically turn to our God who will provide it.

Even after God saved and delivered the Israelites from the hands of their enemies, the Egyptians, through His servant Moses, the Israelites were still mentally, psychologically, emotionally, and spiritually bound to their land of oppression, suppression and depression. God knew this from their thoughts and this became evident in the way and manner they reacted (mostly a negative and faithless reaction), to challenges they faced in the process of their escape from Egypt to the Promised Land.

After the miraculous crossing of the Red Sea by the Israelites, they went into the wilderness of Shur. After a three day journey, they found no water, until they arrived at Marah where they could not drink the water there, because it was bitter. They then murmured against Moses, saying what shall we drink? But the Lord healed the waters to make it sweet for the Israelites to drink. After this episode, the Lord then made a statute and ordinance (rule) for them, tested and promised them through his servant, Moses, that if the Israelites would be obedient to the LORD their God and do His will, He would put none of the diseases upon them, that He brought upon the Egyptians because He is the LORD that healeth them. Now, what better assurance from God could the Israelites had hoped for? This is because they had seen the ten terrible plagues which included sicknesses and diseases that the LORD had visited upon the Egyptians. The Egyptians' gods could not heal them of those sicknesses and diseases, visited upon them by the LORD God.

God's healing power is very much displayed in the earthly ministry of Jesus, God the Son. Of the thirty-seven miracles of Jesus recorded in the New Testament, a whopping twenty-seven of them are about healing, cleansing, deliverance and raising the dead. The healing power of our Lord Jesus Christ in His earthly ministry played a significant part in the salvation of souls.

The outpouring of the Holy Spirit upon the disciples and apostles was manifested by many acts of signs and wonders, with healing forming a significant part of it. Apostles Peter and John were used greatly to perform healing miracles, to the extent that people brought out their sick folks on to the street in Jerusalem so that the shadow of Peter, who was passing by, might fall on them, for their healing.

Today the kingdom of God is full of testimonies of healing of various kinds, physical, psychological, emotional, mental and spiritual. Many believers are being healed of many sicknesses and diseases some of them incurable. Even some believers who died have gone through the "Lazarus" resurrection by being brought back to life. This is confirmation of the fact that the God that we serve is "Jehovah Rophi – The Lord Who Heals You".

Child of God begin to claim by faith that this name of God shall become alive and active in your life day by day. Whenever you feel unwell call upon "The Lord Who Heals You" and He shall send forth His word and heal you as He has declared in Psalm 107:20. "Is any sick among you? Let him call for the elders of the church; and let them pray over him, anointing him with oil in the name of the Lord: And the prayer of faith shall save (heal) the sick and the Lord shall raise him up; and if he has committed sins they shall be forgiven him" (James 5:14-15). This promise is for you and for everyone who has been saved by the blood of Jesus Christ. Make full use of the name of the Lord "Jehovah Rophi".

Fourteen years ago, in 1996, when my wife was pregnant with our second daughter, who happens to be our last child, the scan result showed that the pregnancy was an ectopic pregnancy, and therefore put her life and that of the baby at risk. One night we stood by our faith in the Lord and prayed fervently for the Lord's healing and intervention. As we prayed the Lord revealed to me that the fertilised egg which was wrongly positioned in the fallopian tube was now being moved by the Lord, safely into the womb. I immediately placed my hand on the left side of the lower part of her abdomen and just as I was about to inform her that the fertilised egg was moving from that part of her fallopian tube, she instantly felt a strange sensation in the same area of her body; Praise God, praise Jehovah Rophi "The Lord Who Heals You". My wife had been healed. When she went for her scheduled scan the following morning, the test showed that the fertilised egg had safely been implanted in the womb and that there was no cause for alarm.

Today, by the power of Jehovah Rophi, "The Lord Who Heals You", we have a pretty and lovely daughter. As you read this book now, if you are suffering from any illness or sickness I pray in the name of Jesus who is also "Jehovah Rophi – The Lord Who Heals You", to heal you completely of your sickness or illness. Receive it now in Jesus' name.

Activate the power in this name of God over your life by making the following declaration now and as often as you like:

Oh my soul (say your full name), I arise and receive my healing and deliverance from my Lord Jehovah Rophi (Rapha) for He is my mighty healer. I tap into this powerful name of God for my continuous good health and protection from any attacks in the form of sicknesses and diseases.

CHAPTER SEVENTEEN

JEHOVAH JIRETH (JIREH)

This name of God translates as "The Lord Who Provides".

Genesis 22:1-18 and Matthew 6:19-34.

One of the greatest characteristics of God is the fact that He is a magnificent provider for our needs on a daily basis as well as at critical moments of our lives, spiritually and physically.

Abraham, a man who believed in God and walked in total obedience before Him, at some point, was tested for his faith. He was asked by God to offer Isaac, his only son of promise whom he loved, as a burnt offering for the LORD God in the land of Moriah. Abraham obeyed, took Isaac, the materials needed for the offering and his servants and went on this long journey. He was determined to offer Isaac as a burnt offering in an act of worship to God without any interference from anybody. This is indicated because as they got close to the place where God had asked him to perform the sacrifice, he asked his servants to remain, behind while he and Isaac went to worship the Almighty God. In his heart, he knew he was going to kill Isaac, as a burnt offering to God. When Isaac asked Abraham about the lamb for the offering, he replied that God will provide a lamb, when in his heart, he knew that Isaac was the sacrifice; little did he know that the God, he served, is indeed a God who provides, "Jehovah Jireth". Abraham, after building and preparing the altar for the sacrifice, bound Isaac, his son, and laid him upon the wood, but as he took the knife to slay his son, he was stopped by the angel of the LORD, who provided him with a ram that had been given by God, instead. This led Abraham to name the place Jehovah Jireh.

Every believer must have the full confidence in the power and ability of the God that we serve to be our provider. We should not worry about whether God will meet our needs or not. Instead we should focus on how best we can worship Him through our acts of obedience. Through our acts of obedience to God, we would always experience His power as "Jehovah Jireh", which manifests through the blessings that He gives us. Abraham's obedience to God through his act of worship caused him to see the providing hand of God in his life – Genesis 14:16-18. He was full of trust in God's ability to provide for him in any circumstance to the point that when Isaac asked him about the lamb for the burnt offering, he answered, "The LORD will provide himself a lamb for a burnt offering". Abraham said this when there was no evidence of any such provision for the sacrifice. In much the same way, as believers, let us not wait for any physical evidence of God's provision in our lives, before we trust Him as "Jehovah Jireh". Instead let us focus on our worship of Him all the time.

Jesus teaches us in Matthew 6:24-34 that we should not worry about our daily needs because God, who created us, knows this more than anybody else. In fact He says in Matthew 6:33, "But seek ye first the kingdom of God, and his righteousness; and all these things shall be added unto you". By seeking first the kingdom of God and his righteousness, we make the worshipping of God the most important aspect of our lives, just as Abraham did when he was called upon to sacrifice Isaac for a burnt offering. When we do this, we begin to see the manifestation of the power of God as "Jehovah Jireh" in our lives just as Jesus promised "...and all these things shall be added unto you". Just as Abraham was provided for by God (Jehovah Jireh), even so, can we expect Him to do the same for us as we remain faithful and obedient believers.

Activate the power in this name of God over your life by making the following declaration now and as often as you like:

Oh my soul (say your full name), I know that my self-sufficiency lies in my Lord and God Jehovah Jireth (Jireh). I am assured that my basket will never go empty neither will my well run dry. I trust in Jehovah Jireth and I will never lack anything I need.

CHAPTER EIGHTEEN

JEHOVAH TZADEKENU (TSIDIKENU)

This name of God translates as "The Lord Our Righteousness".

Jeremiah 23:1-6; Romans 1:16-17; Romans 4:6, 20-24 and Romans 6:15-22.

The LORD God is a God of righteousness; hence it has always been His plan to establish His people in a life of His righteousness. Without the Lord's righteousness, no one will be able to draw near to the kingdom of God, and the only way to obtain the Lord's righteousness is through salvation that comes through Jesus Christ. The apostle Paul declared, this emphatically in Romans 1:16-17, "For I am not ashamed of the gospel of Christ: for it is the power of God unto salvation to everyone that believeth; to the Jew first, and also to the Greek. For therein is the righteousness of God revealed from faith to faith: as it is written, THE JUST SHALL LIVE BY FAITH".

Israel, God's chosen nation, lost her way many times and disobeyed God by worshipping other gods and sinned in the process. This brought God's judgment against Israel on a number of occasions, but in the Hebrews' hopeless and helpless state, God still had a plan for them. The plan was to send them a saviour who would take them out of their state of sinfulness, death and destruction, to a new state of righteousness which brings assurance of eternal life and hope.

The book of Romans 6:15-22 explains that because of Christ's death, which paid for our sins, and his resurrection, that guarantees us our eternal life, believers now have the power through Christ to live a new life. In this new life the believer is dead to sin in the sense that they no longer respond to sin like they did before they came to know Christ. They no longer willingly or without shame take pleasure in committing a sin, nor indulge in a lifestyle which made them servants of sin, as is declared in Romans 6:16-18, "Know ye not, that to whom ye yield yourselves servants to obey, his servants ye are to whom ye obey; whether of sin unto death, or of obedience unto righteousness? But God be thanked, that ye were the servants of sin, but ye have obeyed from the heart that form of doctrine which was delivered you. Being then made free from sin, ye became the servants of righteousness".

Therefore by believing in Jesus and taking him as our Lord and saviour, believers have been made free from the stigma or shame of sin and instead have been given a new identity marked by the label of glorious righteousness that comes through faith in Jesus Christ.

David, inspired by the Spirit of God, declared in Psalm 23:3 "He restoreth my soul: he leadeth me in paths of righteousness for his name's sake". David, who was a man after God's own heart and therefore was very intimate with God, had a very rich experience of how the LORD corrected and took his heart away from sin. God guided him in righteous ways and newness of life – ways that would not destroy David and his relationship with God.

As a divine shepherd, the LORD continually guides us (believers) in the ways of righteousness – ways that improve our relationship with God and therefore secures our place in heaven. God is indeed Jehovah Tzadekenu (Tsidikenu) "The Lord Our Righteousness".

Activate the power in this name of God over your life by making the following declaration now and as often as you like:

Oh my soul (say your full name) I have been delivered from the sentence of death to a new life of hope because I have been made righteous by the blood of Jesus. I therefore live my new life in Jesus with confidence for He is The Lord My Righteousness.

CHAPTER NINETEEN

JEHOVAH SHALOM

This name of God translates as "The Lord Is Peace".

Judges 6:24; John 14:27; Luke 8:48; Romans 5:1;
Philippians 4:7; Galatians 5:22; Colossians 1:20; Haggai
2:9; Jeremiah 33:6; Isaiah 26:12 and Psalm 29:11.

When the angel of the LORD visited Gideon and called
him to be the leader of Israel, the nation was constantly
being attacked by the Midianites. The sins of Israel had
led God to deliver them into the hands of Midian for
seven years. Israel never enjoyed peace during this period
as it was under constant attack by the Midianites. Israel
cried out and the LORD responded by choosing a
deliverer in the person of Gideon. The encounter
between the angel of the LORD and Gideon caused
Gideon to feel inadequate, insecure, and afraid that he
might die.

However the LORD reassured him and said, "Peace be
unto thee; fear not thou shalt not die". It was then that
Gideon built an altar there unto the LORD, and called it
Jehovah Shalom "The Lord Is Peace", because he
realised that God is full of peace. Our God is the God of
peace because He is full of peace, and whenever He
comes to us He does so in the name of peace.

The prophecy of the Messiah's birth in Isaiah 9:6-7 clearly shows us the identity and also the nature of Jesus Christ's work. Among Jesus' names is "The Prince of Peace" and that, "Of the increase of His government and peace there shall be no end". From this prophecy we learn that peace is part of the salvation plan that God made for humanity. This is because God Himself is the father and origin of peace. Therefore when the relationship between God and the human race broke down through the disobedience of Adam and Eve, peace as an aspect of life was lost to us. It is therefore, no wonder, that the world, ever since that time, has been full of problems of many kinds and at different levels – spiritual, physical, psychological, emotional, and physiological problems of personal, social, national and global levels.

The world has been crying out for deliverance from all these problems and crises so that it can live a life of peace. When we receive Jesus, as our Lord and saviour, He gives us peace. That is why Jesus declared in John 14:27, "Peace I leave with you, my peace I give unto you: not as the world giveth, give I unto you. Let not your heart be troubled, neither let it be afraid". He is Jehovah Shalom indeed.

Activate the power in this name of God over your life by making the following declaration now and as often as you like:

Oh my soul (say your full name), I remember that the Lord my God is Jehovah Shalom "The Lord Is Peace". Therefore, I enjoy the peace which has come to me as a result of my salvation through Jesus Christ.

CHAPTER TWENTY

JEHOVAH ROHI

This name of God translates as "The Lord My Shepherd".

1 Samuel 17:33-36; Psalm 23; Matthew 18:12-14; John 10:1-16; John 10:27-29; 1 Peter 5:4, and Hebrew 13:20.

A shepherd is someone who looks after or cares for flocks of sheep, goats, cattle, pigs or even other animals that can be domesticated.

Some of the qualities or basic characteristics of a good shepherd are:

1. He feeds his flock on the richest pasture available.
2. He leads his flock to the best rivers, wells or waterholes.
3. He protects his flock against any danger.
4. He is the trustworthy guide to the flock.
5. He cares for the flock when they are ill.
6. He also acts as a midwife to his flock.
7. All these functions of the shepherd make him the sustainer of the flock.

David, inspired by the Holy Spirit, worshipped the Lord in Psalm 23 as his divine shepherd. In this psalm, David expressed his total dependence upon God Almighty. In this psalm, David declared that there was no way he could lead a normal, secure and fruitful life on his own. David confessed to the fact, that with the Lord in control of his life, he had total trust and hope in any circumstance that he found himself in. The Lord meets his physical, spiritual, psychological, emotional needs as well as any other need in his day to day life.

David's expression of full trust in the Lord, as his shepherd, is not at all surprising since part of his teenage life was spent as a shepherd in charge of his father's flock of sheep. Without a shadow of a doubt, he knew the responsibilities a shepherd's role entailed. As a proof of his ability to fight the terrorising Goliath, he explained to Saul, that as a shepherd looking after his father's sheep, he protected the flock from predators like lions and bears by putting his life on the line, fighting and killing these predators all by himself. In 1 Samuel 17:34-35 he said, "...thy servant kept his father's sheep, and there came a lion, and a bear, and took a lamb out of the flock: And I went out after him, and smote him, and delivered it out of his mouth: and when he arose against me, I caught him by his beard, and smote him, and slew him".

David's account of the divine shepherd and his own experience as a shepherd gives a true reflection of our God as our shepherd. In Jesus Christ we find a true shepherd for us, for he says in John 10:11, "I am the good shepherd: the good shepherd giveth his life for the sheep". This verse of scripture is a direct fulfilment of what Isaiah prophesied in Isaiah 53:6, "All we like sheep have gone astray; we have turned everyone to his own way; and the LORD hath laid on him the iniquity of us all". Jesus as the Lamb of God and our shepherd has been made responsible for the washing and the cleansing of our sins so that we would not perish. As a true shepherd he is very much concerned for our eternal destiny to the point that he has provided a protection for us against our eternal condemnation through his sacrificial death upon the cross, so that anyone who obeys the shepherd, gets rescued and protected by his blood, which he shed on the cross.

As members of his flock it is our duty to listen to and obey the voice of our Lord Jesus Christ, our shepherd. Listening to the voice of our shepherd, guarantees us the grace which he offers to us by his death and resurrection. This is what the Lord meant when he declared in John 10:27-28, "My sheep hear my voice, and I know them and they follow me: And I give unto them eternal life; and they shall never perish, neither shall any man pluck them out of my hand". Any sheep that knows the voice of its shepherd and follows his instructions is very safe as it avails itself of the guidance, provision, and the protection that the shepherd offers to his flock. Patience and compassion are great virtues of a shepherd and any shepherd that lacks these virtues will never be successful. Jesus Christ who is our Shepherd is filled with these virtues in abundance that is why His Kingdom will not cease to grow as He never abandons His servants. However any sheep that is continually wayward in their lifestyle and does not follow their shepherd runs the risk of being caught and eaten by predators. Such will be the fate of a sinful believer, a disobedient sheep.

There is a testimony about a neighbour who stole a catechist's sheep from his sheepfold in the vicarage (popularly called Salem in Ghana – a place of peace and no worldly vice), with the intention of selling it to a restaurant in a neighbouring town. Unfortunately for the thief the shepherd (who had noticed that one of his sheep was missing because he was a caring shepherd) boarded the vehicle that the neighbour was using on his fateful journey to the restaurant to sell the sheep. The vehicle was a typical Ghanaian large passenger truck. A drama then unfolded when the sheep heard the voice of its shepherd as he engaged someone in a conversation in another part of the vehicle. The sheep then began to bleat to catch the attention of the unsuspecting shepherd. After a period of continuous bleating, which sounded familiar to the shepherd, the sheep caught the attention of his shepherd who looked towards the direction of the bleating only to see the neighbour sitting nervously, a couple of rows behind him. He then decided to monitor the neighbour's actions afterwards, as to how and when he was going to alight from the vehicle. His suspicion was heightened when the neighbour requested to alight on the outskirts of the bus' destination. As he alighted, the catechist saw him take with him a sheep, so he immediately asked to alight as well, and lo and behold, he discovered to his utter amazement, that the sheep that was bleating all the time was one of his flocks. Before he could even challenge the thief about the sheep, the animal which was on a lead, had already started walking towards him with joy. He was rescued from the hands of a neighbour who led a double life, as a thief and a Christian living in a Salem (a Christian community), which was meant to be a place devoid of any worldly vice. The sheep knew the shepherd's voice and the shepherd knew the sheep's voice so when it bleated for help it was heard and rescued. If it had not been heard and rescued by the shepherd it would have been sold to the restaurant by the thief and then slaughtered. As believers, we need to know the voice of our shepherd and also let the shepherd know our voice through our obedience to him, so that in times of need, when we cry out to him he will hear and answer us, for God is indeed **Jehovah Rohi** "The Lord My Shepherd".

Activate the power in this name of God over your life by making the following declaration now and as often as you like:

Oh my soul (say your full name) I am blessed and highly favoured because the God that I serve is Jehovah Rohi "The Lord My Shepherd". For the omnipotent, omnipresent, and omniscient God to be my eternal shepherd, means there is nothing for me to fear. He has put me in the driver's seat of life; I therefore rejoice and give Him the glory.

CHAPTER TWENTY-ONE

CONCLUSION

The power in the names of God is a heritage for the believer to inherit and use on a daily basis for their benefit. The believer should exercise their faith in the names of God by continually calling upon the appropriate name when faced with any challenge.

Having a strong faith in the names of God is an indication of the nature of the relationship one has with God. The Israelites (Hebrews) experienced the awesome power of God in different dimensions; hence they came up with these names of God to express how they felt about God and how to relate to Him.

As a believer of our Lord Jesus Christ, the meanings of the names of God is absolutely important for holding onto your faith as they point to the fact that these names express that there is salvation in the name of our Lord.

JEHOVAH NISSI – The Lord My Banner. The name of the Lord which is our identification brings us salvation, for the name of the Lord is a strong tower and they that run into it are saved. Acts 10:43, "To Him give all the prophets witness, that through His name whosoever believeth in Him shall receive remission of sins". There is salvation in Jehovah Nissi.

JEHOVAH ROPHI (RAPHA) – The Lord Who Heals You. Jesus' sacrificial death upon the cross brings us healing as well. 1 Peter 2:24, "Who His own self bare our sins in His own body on the tree that we, being dead to sins, should live unto righteousness: by whose stripes ye were healed". There is salvation in Jehovah Rophi (Rapha).

JEHOVAH JIRETH (JIREH) – The Lord Who Provides. Jesus is the bread of life. John 6:57-58, "As the living Father has sent me, and I live by the Father: so he that eateth me, even he shall live by me. This is that bread which came down from heaven: not as your fathers did eat manna, and are dead: he that eateth of this bread shall live forever". There is salvation in Jehovah Jireth.

JEHOVAH TZADEKENU (TSIDIKENU) – The Lord Our Righteousness. Jesus' death and resurrection brought us grace and righteousness before God. Romans 5:17,19, "For if by one man's offence death reigned by one; much more they which receive abundance of grace and of the gift of righteousness shall reign in life by one, Jesus Christ. For as by one man's disobedience many were made sinners, so by the obedience of one shall many be made righteous". There is salvation in Jehovah Tzadekenu (Tsidikenu).

JEHOVAH SHALOM – The Lord Is Peace. The salvation that comes through our Lord Jesus Christ brings us peace. Isaiah 9:6-7, "For unto us a child is born, unto us a son is given: and the government shall be upon His shoulder: and His name shall be called Wonderful, Counsellor, The Mighty God, The everlasting Father, The Prince of Peace. Of the increase of His government and peace there shall be no end, upon the throne of David, and upon His kingdom, to order it, and to establish it with judgment and with justice from henceforth even forever. The zeal of the LORD of hosts will perform this". There is salvation in Jehovah Shalom.

JEHOVAH ROHI – The Lord My Shepherd. As a true shepherd Jesus Christ saves us from the works and attacks of satan and all the evil powers. John 10:10-11, "The thief cometh not, but for to steal, and to kill, and to destroy: I am come that they might have life, and that they might have it more abundantly. I am the good shepherd: the good shepherd giveth his life for the sheep". There is salvation in Jehovah Rohi.

It is my hope that each and every one that reads and studies these names of God prayerfully and also uses them meaningfully, they will have a powerful and lasting impact upon their lives so that those who have a purposeless life will receive a purposeful life, those who are sick and the broken-hearted shall be healed, those who are captives shall be delivered and above all, those who are lost, shall be saved.

God bless you.

Lightning Source UK Ltd.
Milton Keynes UK
UKOW04f1427060214

226009UK00001B/3/P